OUR VALUES

STAYING

SAFE

By Steffi Cavell-Clarke

Crabtree Publishing Company
www.crabtreebooks.com
1-800-387-7650

Published in Canada
Crabtree Publishing
616 Welland Avenue
St. Catharines, ON
L2M 5V6

Published in the United States
Crabtree Publishing
PMB 59051
350 Fifth Ave, 59th Floor
New York, NY 10118

Published by Crabtree Publishing Company in 2018

First Published by Book Life in 2018
Copyright © 2018 Book Life

Author: Steffi Cavell-Clarke

Editors: Kirsty Holmes, Janine Deschenes

Design: Daniel Scase

Proofreader: Petrice Custance

Production coordinator and
  prepress technician (interior): Margaret Amy Salter

Prepress technician (covers): Ken Wright

Print coordinator: Margaret Amy Salter

Photographs
Front cover – Evgeny Bakharev
2 & 3 – Pressmaster. 4 – Rawpixel.com. 5: tl – Monkey Business Images, tm – Tom Wang, tr – Yuliya Evstratenko, mr – Romrodphoto, ml – ESB Professional, br – Lucian Milasan, mb – Pressmaster, bl – amenic181. 6 – VGstockstudio. 7 – Sandra Gligorijevic. 8 – wavebreakmedia. 9 – wavebreakmedia. 10: l – Filimages, b – Brian A Jackson, r – 1000 words. 11 – littlekidmoment. 12 – Daniel Jedzura. 13 – Rad K. 14 – Daxiao Productions. 15 – l i g h t p o e t. 16 – Manoonson Sonon. 17 – Edler von Rabenstein. 18 – Monkey Business Images. 19 – Syda Productions. 20 – wavebreakmedia. 21 – Dawn Shearer-Simonetti. 22 – Pressmaster. 23 – Dmitry Kalinovsky. Images are courtesy of Shutterstock.com. With thanks to Getty Images, Thinkstock Photo and iStockphoto.

Printed in the USA/012018/BG20171102

Library and Archives Canada Cataloguing in Publication

Cavell-Clarke, Steffi, author
    Staying safe / Steffi Cavell-Clarke.

(Our values)
Includes index.
Issued in print and electronic formats.
ISBN 978-0-7787-4730-7 (hardcover).--
ISBN 978-0-7787-4745-1 (softcover).--
ISBN 978-1-4271-2083-0 (HTML)

    1. Safety education--Juvenile literature. I. Title.

HQ770.7.C38 2018   j613.6083   C2017-906921-7
                                             C2017-906922-5

Library of Congress Cataloging-in-Publication Data

CIP available at the Library of Congress

CONTENTS

Words that are in bold, like **this**, can be found in the glossary on page 24.

WHAT ARE VALUES?

Values are the things you believe are important, such as caring for the environment. The ways we think and behave depend on our values. They help us learn how to **respect** each other and ourselves. Sharing the same values as others helps us live and work together in a **community**.

Being responsible

Making safe choices

Making friends

Our Values

Respecting the law

Telling the truth

Caring for the environment

STAYING SAFE

You are cared for by your parents, guardians, teachers, and other trusted adults. These people make sure that you are always safe. However, you also need to take responsibility for, or look after, your own safety.

Being safe means that you do not put yourself or other people in danger. You make safe choices by thinking about the **outcomes** of different actions. Being safe also means that you stay aware of what is happening around you.

WHY IS IT IMPORTANT?

It is very important to look after your own safety because it will **prevent** you from getting hurt. Understanding the dangers around you at school, at home, and in your community means that you will be able to make safe decisions.

When you ride a bike, skateboard, or scooter outside, falling down is a danger. You can stay safe by choosing to wear a helmet.

If you feel unsafe or notice something that you think is a danger to yourself or others, it is important that you tell a trusted, responsible adult, such as a parent, guardian, or teacher. They will be able to help you so that you feel safe again.

EMERGENCY SERVICES

An emergency is when there is a serious **accident** and people are hurt or in danger. Emergencies are usually unexpected and need quick action. There are different emergency services that can help. The people below are trained to help people who are hurt in emergencies, and keep others safe.

Firefighter

Paramedic

Police Officer

If you are ever in an emergency, call emergency services right away. In the United States and Canada, this number is 911. Listen to what the **telephone operator** asks you to do and answer them as clearly as possible. Do not hang up until they tell you to. It is important to stay calm and wait for help to arrive.

Do not call 911 if there is not an emergency.

SAFETY AT HOME

Many people feel safe at home, but accidents can still happen there. By being responsible and following a few basic tips, you can make sure that you and the people you live with are safe.

Share these safety tips with your parents or guardians, and make sure to follow any safety rules they set at home:

- Never touch **electrical** outlets

- Never put metal items, such as forks and knives, in toasters

- Never use electrical items, such as hair dryers, around water

- Never use matches, candles, or kitchen appliances, such as the stove, without an adult present

- Do not answer the door if you are home alone, or if a stranger, or someone you do not know, is there

°F

13

SAFETY IN PUBLIC

When you are out in public, you always need to be aware of your surroundings. Pay attention to what others are doing around you. Look around your environment for things that might be unsafe. Follow signs that you see, and rules that you are told.

Signs and road markings such as these tell you where, and when, to safely cross roads.

It is important to be careful around strangers, or people you do not know. Most people are kind and helpful, but some strangers could make you feel unsafe. Talk to your parents, guardians, or other trusted adults about how you should deal with strangers. You should never go anywhere with a stranger.

ANIMAL SAFETY

Animals are living things and should be treated with respect. It is important to be careful around animals, and never hurt them. Most pets enjoy playing and being with people, but not all pets are the same. Even a friendly pet could bite if it feels scared or hurt.

Not all animals are pets. Be careful around any animal you see outside.

Riley was walking through town with his older sister when he saw a dog sitting outside a store. Riley wanted to pet the dog, but his older sister told him not to. She explained to Riley that they did not know if the dog was dangerous.

Never touch an animal that you do not know, unless a trusted adult says it is okay.

ONLINE SAFETY

Playing and talking to your friends online can be fun, but it is very important to make sure you are safe. Talk to your parent, guardian, or teacher at school about using a computer safely. Only use websites that they tell you are safe to use. Ask questions if you are not sure.

You may meet and speak to people online that you haven't met in person. It may feel like you are good friends with them, but it is important to remember they are still strangers. You should never share personal information, such as your full name, photo, phone number, or address, with strangers online.

Always tell a parent, guardian, or other trusted adult if you feel unsafe while playing or talking online.

PEER PRESSURE

Your friends are important parts of your life. You may spend a lot of time with them. Remember that it is important to be safe when you spend time with your friends. Sometimes, your friends may do something that you think is unsafe. You may feel **pressured** to participate.

Even if you feel pressured, or want to make your friends happy, it is important to say no when you think that something is unsafe. If your friends tease you or try to make you do something unsafe, you should leave and ask a trusted adult to come and get you.

TAKING MEDICINE

When we become sick, we sometimes need to take **medicine** to help us get better. Doctors can give us medicine when we need it. They are the only people who can tell us if it is safe to take medicine.

You should never take medicine unless your parent or guardian is there with you. They help make sure you are safe by giving you the right dose, or amount, of the medicine. Never take other people's medicine, or give your medicine to someone else. This is unsafe.

GLOSSARY

accident [AK-si-d*uh* nt] An unexpected event that causes damage or injury

community [k*uh*-MYOO-ni-tee] A group of people who live, work, and play in a place

electrical [ih-LEK-tri-k*uh* l] Something that uses electricity to work

environment [en-VAHY-r*uh* n m*uh* nt] Your surroundings

law [law] Rules made by government that a community has to follow

medicine [MED-*uh*-sin] A liquid or pill that treats an illness

outcomes [OUT-kuhms] The results of an action or process

paramedic [par-*uh*-MED-ik] Also called an Emergency Medical Technician or EMT, a paramedic provides emergency medical services by responding to emergency calls

pressured [PRESH-er-ed] Trying to force someone to do something

prevent [pri-VENT] To stop something from happening

respect [ri-SPEKT] Giving something or someone the attention it deserves

responsible [ri-spon-suh-buhl] Reliable or dependable

telephone operator [TEL-*uh*-fohn OP-*uh*-rey-ter] A person whose job it is to answer the phone and speak to the caller

INDEX